Visions
Of
Lent

Lenten Congregational
Resources
Volume 3

Betty Lynn Schwa'

CSS Publishing Company, Inc.
Lima, Ohio

Copyright © 1996 by
CSS Publishing Company, Inc.
Lima, Ohio

ISBN: 0-7880-0227-9   PRINTED IN U.S.A.

Proudly and lovingly
dedicated to

David

who
joyfully and enthusiastically
is harvesting his own
First Fruits

and who finds each one of them
drawing him
more wonderfully yet

into God

Table Of Contents

Introduction

*You shall keep the festival of weeks for the Lord your
God, contributing a freewill offering in proportion to the
blessing that you have received from the Lord your God.*
— Deuteronomy 16:10

Shavuot or the Festival of Weeks is the least known of the
three Jewish pilgrimage festivals observed faithfully by Jewish families in Jesus' day. The other two pilgrimage festivals
are the Festival of Passover (Pesach) and the Festival of Booths
(Sukkot). Chronologically, Shavuot comes between Passover
(see *Visions Of Lent, Year One*) and Booths (see *Visions Of
Lent, Volume Two*). Shavuot falls seven weeks after Passover.
It is also known as the Feast of Harvest (Leviticus 23:15-21)
and Festival of the First Fruits (Exodus 23:16, 17; 34:22).

What does Shavuot have to do with us and our season of
Lent?

Shavuot, like Passover and Sukkot, was one reason why
Jesus would have "gone up to" Jerusalem just prior to the
events of Holy Week. As the disciples and Gospel writers later
wrestled with the meaning of Christ's suffering and death, they
drew upon significant truths encapsulated in their Jewish festivals. Through these truths, they gradually discovered deeper meaning in the life and death of Jesus Christ. They came
to understand the Christ Event as a significant reinterpretation of their Festival of Passover, their Festival of Booths and

7

their Festival of Shavuot. By focussing on some of the elements of these festivals, we can discover in turn deeper insight into the Jesus of history and the Christ of faith.

While standing independent of the first two volumes in this series, this worship resource builds upon some of the groundwork laid for Year One and for Volume Two of this three-part series. This worship resource takes seriously the modern context of Lent as outlined in the introductions of those earlier resources. It also follows, in general, the liturgical patterns of those resources.

In some ways these services may appear new or unusual for Lent. They certainly are different from traditional Lenten liturgies. Yet, at a deeper level, the faith issues of these resources emerge as the same as traditional services: our unworthiness before God, our gratitude to God for Jesus Christ, and our deep sense of awe as we contemplate the events of the last week in the earthly life of Jesus Christ.

The Festival of Shavuot has a very interesting history. At the time of Jesus' life on earth, it had not crystallized as much as the Festivals of Passover and Booths. Yet Shavuot was diligently observed at the Temple, honoring and expressing its original agricultural roots, while pointing to its emerging secondary theme.

While the Gospels were being written, and especially after the Temple at Jerusalem was destroyed in 70 A.D., the Festival of Shavuot underwent an enormously significant reinterpretation for the Jewish people. That reinterpretation played directly into the hands of the Gospel writers. With the temple gone, the primary agricultural theme gave way to the emergent secondary theme: God's giving of the Torah to the People of Israel. Thus as the members of the Jewish community were reflecting seriously on the meaning of the Torah and how it was given to them as the People of God, so the Gospel writers were reflecting seriously on the meaning of Christ and how he came to the People of God. For Christians today the various aspects of the Festival of Shavuot — both its agricultural and Torah themes — bring new focus to details within the Holy

Week narrations, details that seem puzzling, odd, or unconnected, and yet were preserved in the Christian Sacred Story.

Preparation for this worship series is very simple. We begin on the eve of Lent 1, filling the sanctuary as full as possible with greenery. Following a Jewish Shavuot custom, each family in the congregation is invited to lend a plant from home (silk or live). Plants and flowers of all kinds are welcome. A suggested bulletin insert and sample visual reminder to use for a few weeks prior to the eve of Lent 1 are included in this resource. A focal point needs to be created with some (if not all) of this greenery somewhere at the front of the sanctuary. This is easily done using an inexpensive trellis. (We tied one to an unused microphone stand!) Attach silk flowers and greenery to it with tie tapes and arrange the congregation's plants gracefully around it. An object is added each week in or around this focal point as follows:

Lent 1: a big basket abundantly full of fresh and/or artificial fruit of all kinds

Lent 2: two unsliced loaves of bread

Lent 3: a large pitcher of water (a large baptismal shell may also be placed in the focal area before the service begins and large crystal teardrop prisms hung from the trellis). The baptismal font should be nearby.

Lent 4: the congregational Bible or a family-size Bible (to be placed in the focal point by a member of the congregation, elder or usher when all have received it)

Lent 5: a small, simple wooden cross

Palm/Passion Sunday (Lent 6): a large red heart (such as cut from bristol board) with a large cross drawn clearly or cut out in the middle of the heart. Palm branches and crosses could also be distributed to the congregation as they come in and palm branches and fronds added to the focal area prior to the service beginning.

The arrangement of these objects will be quite different for each congregation. Simple beauty is always the key.

Two readers (youth or adult) carry the dialogue each week, with a third person (possibly a young child) holding the week's object during the dialogue and placing the object in the focal point on a previously arranged spot after the congregational prayer. These three may change each week or remain the same for the six weeks. We chose to have a different family involved each week, letting each family decide who would like to read and who would simply hold the visual object and place it in the focal point when the prayer was ended. When possible, the family was also invited to prepare and bring the object added to the display each week. Do be careful to choose your best readers! Coach them to read slowly, looking up as much as possible at the congregation.

The entire script need not be included in the congregation's weekly bulletin. Include instead only the scripture read by Reader 1 followed by a short series of periods or dots and then the phrase, "Let us pray," followed by the congregational prayer. (See the Order of Service for Palm/Passion Sunday in this resource.)

This resource includes a suggested order of service for Palm/Passion Sunday. This service includes the lectionary Gospel reading for the day and builds upon the themes of Lent 1 to Palm/Passion Sunday. The Lenten resource for Palm/Passion Sunday is not dependent upon the included worship service. But this worship service is dependent, at least in part, upon the ideas developed from Lent 1 to Palm/Passion Sunday in this resource.

May the God who calls to us today out of some of the most ancient passages in our Holy Scripture fill your Festival of Weeks with the Holy Spirit and may the First Fruits and Harvest of your Lenten season this year be richly and abundantly Christ-like.

**SHAVUOT
IS
COMING!**

This year, we will celebrate Lent by sharing in the third Jewish pilgrimage festival that would have brought Jesus to Jerusalem — the festival of Shavuot.

To decorate our sanctuary, you are invited to bring a plant(s) from home, real or silk. Be sure your name is on the pot! Please bring your plants by (insert a date here)!

Hag Sameach!

An example of a plant reminder

Somewhere in the narthex or welcoming area of your church a visual focus like this will pique curiosity and help remind people to bring their plant(s) in!

Sample Torah for bulletin inserts

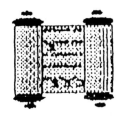

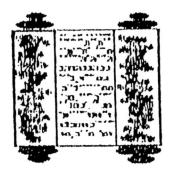

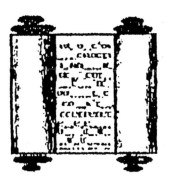

Sample labels for focal display

Instructions:
1. Photocopy sheets. Enlarge, if necessary or desired.

2. Cut apart each of the six labels.

3. Glue each strip to a slightly larger strip of purple construction paper.

4. Place near object added each week (see Example of Completed Shavuot Display on page 42).

Lent 3   Waters of Faith

Lent 2   The Bread of Life

Lent 1   First Fruits

Lent 6   Self-emptying Love

Lent 5   The Covenant of Redemption

Lent 4   The Word of God Received

Lent 1

Reader 1: God spoke to Moses saying: "You shall keep the Festival of Shavuot for the Lord your God, contributing a free-will offering in proportion to the blessing that you have received from the Lord."

Reader 2: In Jesus' day, the Festival of Shavuot required every male in Israel to travel to the Temple of Jerusalem. There he offered God the first ripe fruits of this land. It was a time of thanksgiving for the goodness of the land. On Shavuot, it was said, Heaven decided the fate of the trees and crops, so the people prayed for good harvest, for abundant fruit on their trees and vines.

Reader 1: From ancient times the celebration of Shavuot included decorating the synagogues and homes with green plants, branches, trees and flowers. This was a reminder of the first fruits taken to the Temple.

Reader 2: When the Temple in Jerusalem was destroyed, the Gospel writers remembered Jesus' words about first fruits that Jesus spoke during his last days.

Reader 1: After his triumphal entry into Jerusalem, Jesus was hungry. He looked at a fig tree for food and found no fruit. He cursed the tree and it withered. After this, he washed the Apostles' feet and told them about his betrayal and death. Then Jesus said that he was the True Vine and that those who abided in him would bear much fruit. Those who did not abide in him would be cast off like a pruned branch and wither away.

Reader 2: During our season of Lent, the Festival of Shavuot calls to us out of the most ancient passages of our Old

Testament. Do you recognize your own dependence upon the environment today? Do you take time to express sincere thanks to God for God's blessing upon your life? What fruit does your life bear because of your faith in Christ Jesus?

Reader 1: Let us pray.

All: God of the Heavens and Earth, you blessed Ancient Israel, Jesus and the Apostles. You bless us today. During Lent this year, help us to be more mindful of your presence in our lives. May we be moved more often to give you thanks. May our daily life bear more fruit because of our faith in Christ. Amen.

Lent 1 Presentation Symbol

Lent 2

Reader 1: God spoke to Moses saying: "You shall keep the Festival of Shavuot for the Lord your God, contributing a free-will offering in proportion to the blessing that you have received from the Lord."

Reader 2: In Jesus' day, the Festival of Shavuot required every male in Israel to travel to the Temple of Jerusalem. There he offered God the gift of baked bread. Shavuot was the only time an offering was made from leavened flour. Two well-prepared loaves of bread were waved before the altar. These loaves were made from the finest wheat grown by the family that year. After this the new season's wheat could be used for other offerings. Bread was thus a sign of recognition.

Reader 1: When we look at the stories about Jesus' last days, bread plays an important role. Jesus used bread to explain the meaning of his death: "While they were eating, he took a loaf of bread and blessed it, broke it, and gave it to them saying, 'Take this, this is my body given for you.' " Bread was a sign of sacrifice.

Reader 2: Bread was also a sign of betrayal. Psalm 41:9 says "Even my bosom friend ... who ate of my bread" has betrayed me. After Jesus told the disciples about his betrayal, he dipped a piece of bread and gave it to Judas Iscariot. After eating this bread, Judas went out and betrayed Jesus to the religious authority of his day. Bread was a sign of betrayal.

Reader 1: The ancient Festival of Shavuot teaches us an important lesson. Any event in our life, even the simplest object or action in our daily living, can draw us closer to God or move us away from God.

Reader 2: When you look at bread this week, what will you see? Will you see a reminder of God's participation in our agricultural industry? Will you see a reminder of Christ's immense love for you? Will you see an invitation for you to live a sacramental life? Will you see a reminder that at any moment each of us can betray the best of human living?

Reader 1: Let us pray.

All: Holy God, we know Jesus is the Bread of Life and that we are called by him to be the Bread of Life in our world today. Make us alert to the ordinary details of our daily life. Help us learn to see these details as tools for our Christian faith. Amen.

Lent 2 Presentation Symbol

Lent 2   The Bread of Life

Lent 3

Reader 1: God spoke to Moses saying: "You shall keep the Festival of Shavuot for the Lord your God, contributing a free-will offering in proportion to the blessing that you have received from the Lord."

Reader 2: In earliest times, during the Festival of Shavuot the Jewish people sprinkled their gardens and fields with symbolic drops of water. This was done so the gardens and fields would yield good harvests. This sprinkling was a gesture of hope. It showed their belief in the goodness of God. At times the sprinkling became a joyful celebration. People sprinkled one another and lucky passersby!

Reader 1: Symbolic droplets are also part of the story of Jesus' last days. On the night of his betrayal, Jesus went out to the Mount of Olives to pray. Scripture says that as Jesus prayed, his sweat became like great drops of blood falling down on the ground. Scripture also says that as Jesus walked to his crucifixion, women wept for him. Jesus urged them not to weep for him but for themselves. The wood — he said — was green that day. But one day it would be dry and it would need their tears then.

Reader 2: Later Jesus hung on the cross. A soldier pierced Jesus' side. Out of Jesus' side poured blood and water in drops upon the ground.

Reader 1: Blessed and sprinkled, the gardens and fields of ancient Israel yielded abundant fruit.

Reader 2: Having prayed as Jesus did, Jesus was able to be faithful to God — even though that meant death upon a cross.

Reader 1: For you and me today, the whole earth has been touched with the water and blood of Christ. Now it is our turn to be faithful to God.

(Person holding pitcher of water pours dramatically into font or large dish and places pitcher in the focal area.)

Reader 2: Let us pray.

All: God of the rains, God of our teardrops, God of baptismal fonts everywhere, we know you call to us. We know we need to stop and pay attention to you. When water next splashes in our font, when raindrops fall upon our head, when a tear slips down our cheeks, help us turn to you and follow you as the women did. Help us draw strength from you as Jesus did. Help us see abundant fruit grow because of our Christian faith today. Amen.

Lent 3 Presentation Symbol

Lent 4

Reader 1: God spoke to Moses saying: "You shall keep the Festival of Shavuot for the Lord your God, contributing a free-will offering in proportion to the blessing that you have received from the Lord."

Reader 2: Shavuot was an agricultural festival. The people recognized God's greatness because of the first fruits and grain God provided through God's gift of land. But Shavuot had a deeper meaning for the people of God in Jesus' day. For the greatest gift of God to God's people was the gift of the Torah, the Old Testament, revealed in glory to Moses on Mount Sinai.

Reader 1: Shavuot thus celebrates the most important event in Jewish history. The Old Testament is not just laws but destiny, not just literature but essence, not just speculation but revelation. God gave this revelation to the people. Their role was to receive it.

Reader 2: Sometimes, out of great respect for the Old Testament, the Jewish people celebrate Shavuot by passing their Torah to each member of the congregation. This gesture symbolizes how each member must personally receive the Word of God into his/her own life and personally strive to live up to the Revelation. For centuries it has been a custom for Jewish people to stay up the whole night before Shavuot. During the night they study the Torah to show their commitment to God and their desire to receive God's commandments.

Reader 1: As Christians, the words easily slip across our lips that Jesus is the Word of God and that the Bible is a holy record of God's revelation to us. In this season of Lent, let us pause to reflect on those truths. How do you show respect and love for the Bible in your home and in your life? *(Pause)* Would you please stand?

All: We, the People of God today, publicly recognize that we do not always hold our Bible in high regard. It gets buried under magazines on the coffee table. It gathers dust on a bookshelf. Some of us may not even own a modern version of it. We recognize, too, that we take for granted the Truth our Bible offers us today. Beginning this week, we resolve to read our Bible more faithfully and to reflect the Bible's Truth better in our daily living. God is our witness! May God help us live out this resolve!

Reader 2: As a symbol of the statement we have just made, throughout the service this morning we will pass to one another our congregational Bible. As you pass it to your neighbor say, "Receive the Word of God," and as you receive it from your neighbor respond, "Amen."

Lent 4 Presentation Symbol

Lent 5

Reader 1: God spoke to Moses saying: "You shall keep the Festival of Shavuot for the Lord your God, contributing a free-will offering in proportion to the blessing that you have received from the Lord."

Reader 2: Shavuot was an agricultural holiday. The people recognized the goodness of God because of the food God provides through God's gift of land. But Shavuot had a deeper meaning for the people of God in Jesus' day. The greatest gift of God to the people was the gift of the Torah, the Law revealed in great glory to Moses on Mount Sinai.

Reader 1: So Shavuot celebrates the most important event in Jewish history: the giving of God's Law on Mount Sinai. This Law was freely given in an ownerless place, the desert. This Law was accepted by the people. It bound the people to God and God to the people.

Reader 2: Shavuot is therefore also called the Festival of the Covenant of Redemption. Through the Law, the people entered into partnership with God to help bring about God's kind of world here on earth.

Reader 1: Before he died, Jesus revealed his commandment to the disciples: "Love one another as I have loved you." He also revealed that just as God disappeared from Moses' sight, so Jesus would disappear from the disciples' sight through his painful death. Jesus' own life was freely given in an ownerless place we call Golgotha, the Place of the Skull.

Reader 2: This new revelation was rejected by Peter. All the Apostles abandoned Christ. Yet in Christ's death a new Covenant of Redemption was born.

Reader 1: As Christ's Covenant People, we are in partnership with Christ today, working as his community of faith to bring about Christ's vision of life in our world.

Reader 2: Let us pray.

All: Jesus Christ, freely God gives and freely you gave. Help us in turn to freely give ourselves to you. Help us grow in our faith. Help us also to freely give ourselves to our own community of faith so that your Covenant of Redemption may be boldly lived out in our neighborhood today. Amen.

Lent 5 Presentation Symbol

Lent 5: The Covenant of Redemption

Palm/Passion Sunday
[Lent 6]

Reader 1: God spoke to Moses saying: "You shall keep the festival of Shavuot for the Lord your God, contributing a free-will offering in proportion to the blessing that you have received from the Lord."

Reader 2: The two Shavuot themes of harvest and revelation come together in the Old Testament Book of Ruth. For this reason the Book of Ruth is read during Shavuot. Ruth was a Moabite woman who had married an Israelite man who lived in Moab. He soon died. When Ruth's mother-in-law decided to return to her homeland of Israel, Ruth boldly said, "Where you go, I will go; where you lodge, I will lodge. Your people will be my people and your God shall be my God." So Ruth moved from Moab to Bethlehem. Out of her lineage came King David and in time Jesus Christ.

Reader 1: As they sat together in the Upper Room, Jesus had his final conversation with the disciples. He said that where he was going the disciples could not go. He also said they knew the way to go. He had to go away — he said — in order to prepare a place for them but he would not leave them feeling alone.

Reader 2: Thomas replied that they didn't understand. Where was Jesus going? How could the disciples possibly know the way? Jesus said he was the way, the truth and the life. If the disciples wanted to abide in him, and he in them, they were to love one another as he loved them. Then Jesus prayed that his disciples would be one just as he and God were one.

Reader 1: The festival of Shavuot calls on all Christians to balance the Law and the Love of God. Faith without love is empty at its core. Love without obedient faith has no depth. Jesus Christ shows us how to live out truly loving faith and truly faith-filled love. Jesus is our way into union with God. Jesus shows us how to be Ruth today.

Reader 2: Let us pray.

All: God of Palm Sunday, you are also God of the Passion. This Holy Week help us remember Jesus' death and Jesus' love. Help us to experience loving faith and faith-filled love. May all our life become a freewill offering in proportion to the blessings we receive from you. In the name of the one who rode the donkey and hung on the cross, Jesus Christ. Amen.

Palm/Passion Sunday Presentation Symbol

Example of the Completed Shavuot Display

About The Palm/Passion Sunday Worship Service

In many churches, most of the congregation come to the Palm Sunday worship service but fewer to the Maundy Thursday and/or Good Friday service(s). Many worshippers, therefore, move from Palm Sunday to Easter Sunday and thus miss the depth of Easter's meaning. For this reason, the order of service which follows celebrates both the Palm Sunday theme and the Passion of Jesus.

This order of service opens with a celebration of the Palm Sunday parade. Let this part of the service be joyful, colorful and noisy. The Musical Prelude, for example, is a suitable time for trumpet or other brass sounds. A trumpet could accompany the first two hymns. Have both Palm Sunday Parade scripture readings read enthusiastically. The Church School Hymn assumes the children attend the service up to that point and then leave for their private time as that hymn plays. The Prayer of Confession after the Church School Hymn marks the shift from the Palm Sunday to Passion Sunday themes.

In denominations where the Eucharist is a regular part of Sunday worship, it is suggested that it be inserted after the offering and before the Prayer of Confession. This Eucharist would, therefore, take on a Palm Sunday celebratory tone, leaving the somber passion tone to the Eucharist celebrated on Maundy Thursday or Good Friday.

The scripture readings should flow unannounced as well as the prayers of response, anthems and hymns. The readings given are the Gospel texts for Year C of the Revised Common Lectionary. Year A or B may easily be substituted, or any combination of the three.

No matter what lectionary year it is, the Lesson from the Gospel is so powerful that it stands on its own. No further comments or explanations are needed at all. Ensure that there are excellent readers for this part of the service. Let the story be read with all the expression and emotion it deserves. It probably works best and easiest to alternate the readings between two readers. A quiet, yet expressive female voice could alternate with a dramatic, strong, male voice.

A visual focal point completes the Gospel reading. This can be accomplished in either of two ways depending on your sanctuary.

The simplest way is to arrange a small series of objects from the Gospel readings around the communion table, separate from the Lenten garden focal point. These objects might include a communion pitcher, plate, a loaf of bread and chalice, a ceramic rooster, a crown of thorns, or a royal robe.

A second way to develop a focal point is to have a group of two or three take up poses symbolizing the events of the story. For example, one man would lift up the communion bread as if offering it to the congregation for Luke 22:14-38 or kneel as in prayer for Luke 22:39-62. Let the "actors" chose which events to pose, and silently flow from one pose to another within a single reading, holding each pose for a few moments as the passage is read. An understated series of a few silent poses is very effective. No costumes underscores the fact that the Passion story could very well happen all over again in our time and place. Let there be a moment of silence between each reading and prayer and hymn/anthem. A postlude is not indicated or needed.

Example of a Palm/Passion Sunday focal point

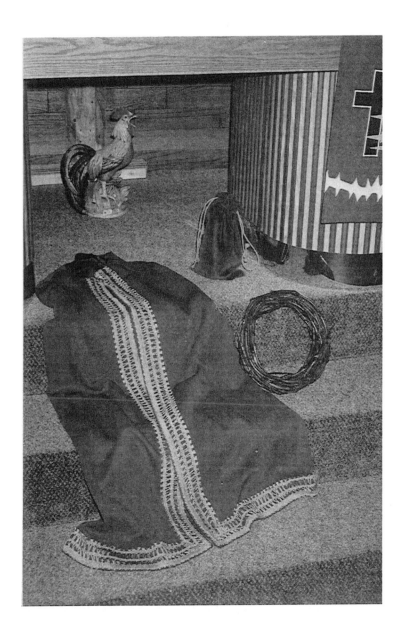

Order Of Service
Palm/Passion Sunday

Musical Prelude
As the prelude plays, parents and children ages 3-7 are invited to line up at the sanctuary for our Palm Sunday Parade

Entering Jerusalem: Luke 19:29-38

Call To Worship (Based on Psalm 118)

One: This is God's day! Let us be happy! Let us celebrate!

Choir: God bless the One who comes in the name of the Lord!

All: Hosanna! Hosanna! Hosanna in the highest!

One: With branches in your hand, start the festival! Wave the branches high and come into God's sanctuary singing!

Choir: Hosanna! Hosanna!

All: Hosanna in the highest! Blessed is He who comes in the name of God! Hosanna!

Processional Hymn: "Hosanna, Loud Hosanna"

Prayer Of Approach *(in unison)*
>God of Palms and crosses, God of sacred parades and holy
>festivals, we worship you!
>Today is Palm Sunday! Your Son Jesus Christ, is truly Lord
>of lords, King of kings!
>Jesus Christ came in your holy name!
>>We come now in His name.
>>Help us to worship you
>>>this holy festive day! Amen!

Announcements

Anthem

Visions Of Shavuot

Reader 1: God spoke to Moses . . .

Reader 2: . . . let us pray.

All: God of Palm Sunday, you are also God of the Passion. This Holy Week help us remember Jesus' death and Jesus' love. Help us to experience loving faith and faith-filled love. May all our life become a free-will offering in proportion to the blessings we receive from you. In the name of the one who rode the donkey and hung on the cross, Jesus Christ. Amen.

Call For The Offering

One: Our King is truly here!

All: Let us worship Him with gifts worthy of God.

One: The offering will now be received.

Offering

Offering Dedication (Tune: 8888 or Old 100th):
We bring our gifts, oh Holy One,
To honor you this Day of Palms.
Bless them we pray in Jesus' name,
Our King, Our Guide, Our Friend, Our Lord.
Amen.

Conclusion Of The Palm Sunday Parade: Luke 19:39-44

Church School Hymn: "Ride On! Ride On In Majesty!"
(vv. 1, 3, 5)

Prayer Of Confession
God of the Heavens and Earth, you ask us to bear fruit for you and to dedicate all our first fruits to you. So your people did in the Temple times long ago. Joyfully they carried to you baskets of first fruits and sheaves of first wheats harvested each year. Yet they failed to recognize Jesus.

We fail to bear fruit for you in our daily living. We do not really dedicate much to you of our daily bread. We too fail to recognize how you are trying to save us. Forgive us, God. Amen.

In The Upper Room: Luke 22:14-38

Our Prayer Of Response
God of Life and Death, you hold out to us the Bread of Life. We accept it easily each service of communion. Then, having eaten at your table, we go out into the world and in many subtle, different ways try to be the greatest. We, like Peter, think we are travelling your way through life. But are we, Lord? Are you saying to us also, "That is enough!"? Break for us again the Bread of Life and help us see all our living as a sacramental life. Amen.

Anthem

In The Garden: Luke 22:39-62

49

Our Prayer Of Response

God of our teardrops and every drop of blood shed, even Christ knew how difficult it is to be faithful to you. Christ sweated drops of blood in prayer, seeking your guidance and strength. Peter wept bitterly, knowing he betrayed Jesus.

All of us know what it is to weep in fear, in pain or in confusion, alone or with others. All of us know we can be better people. When water next splashes in our font, when raindrops fall on us, when a tear slips down our cheeks, help us turn to you again and find strength, guidance and peace. Amen.

Hymn: "Man Of Sorrows" (vv. 1, 2, 4)

The Sentencing: Luke 22:63—23:25

A Prayer Of Response

Holy God, your greatest gift to us is the Word of Life. Whenever we really read or listen to it, Your Word comes to life. Your Word is not just Law but Destiny. Your Word is not just Speculation but Revelation.

Today two words ring in our ears: Crucify Him! Crucify Him! Let us not take this story lightly nor Christ for granted. Help us give thanks to you for Him and then to work everywhere and always to stop these words from being shouted yet again. Amen.

The Crucifixion: Luke 23:26-43

Hymn: "Beneath The Cross"

Our Prayer Of Response

Jesus Christ, freely God gives and freely you gave. May we in turn give ourselves more fully and more freely to you until we too are in Paradise with you. Amen.

The Death And Burial: Luke 23:44-56

50

Commissioning And Benediction

One: The God of Palm Sunday's joyful parade is the God of the dreadful place called "The Skull."

All: May we be mindful of the power of Jesus' life — and death — this Holy Week.

One: Go forth confident in the Creator's love, secure in Christ's strength and comforted by the Spirit's presence.

All: May loving faith and faith-filled love be the spice and perfume of our life this week. Amen.

The congregation is asked to remain seated a few moments in silence and to leave quietly when each feels ready.